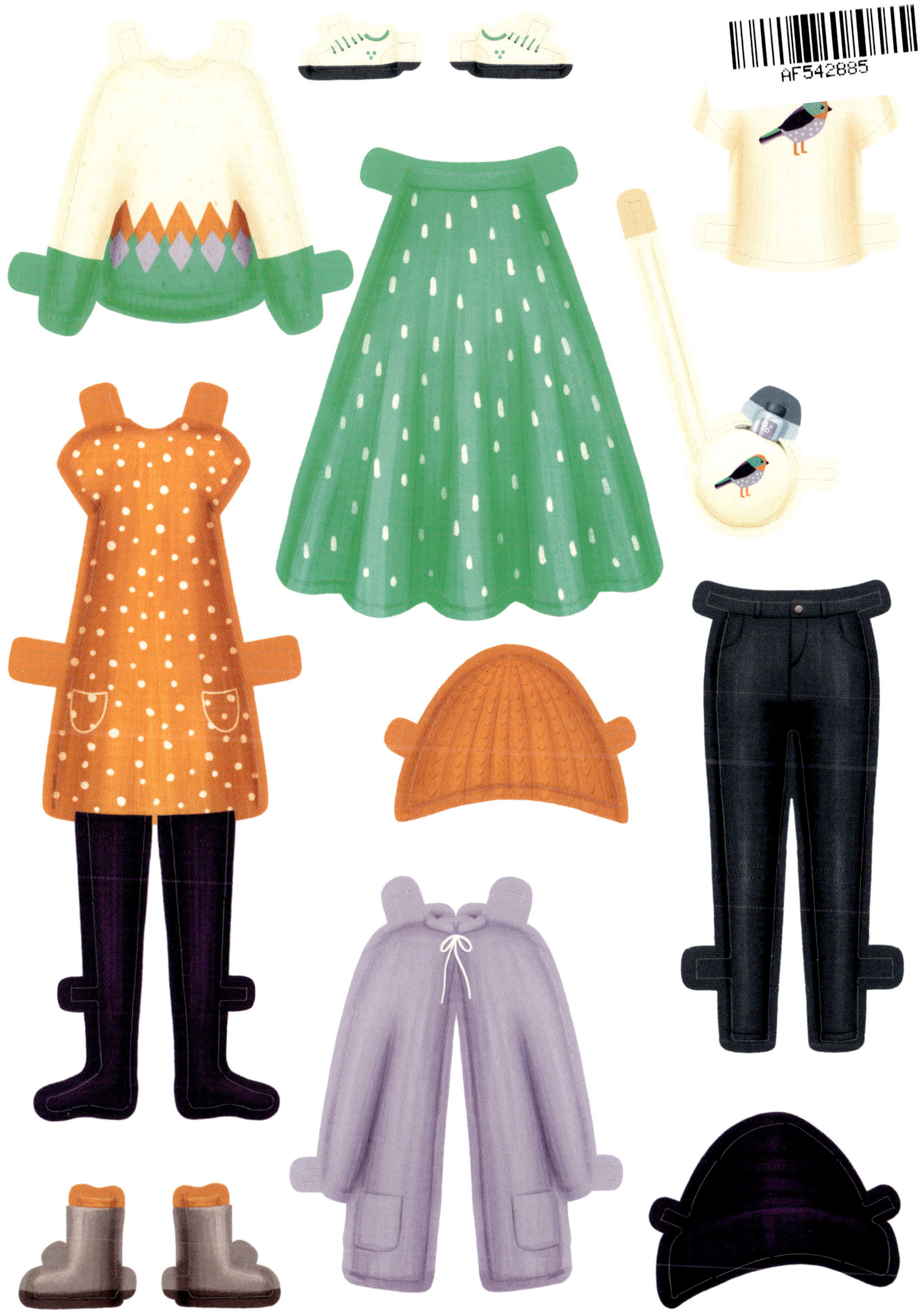

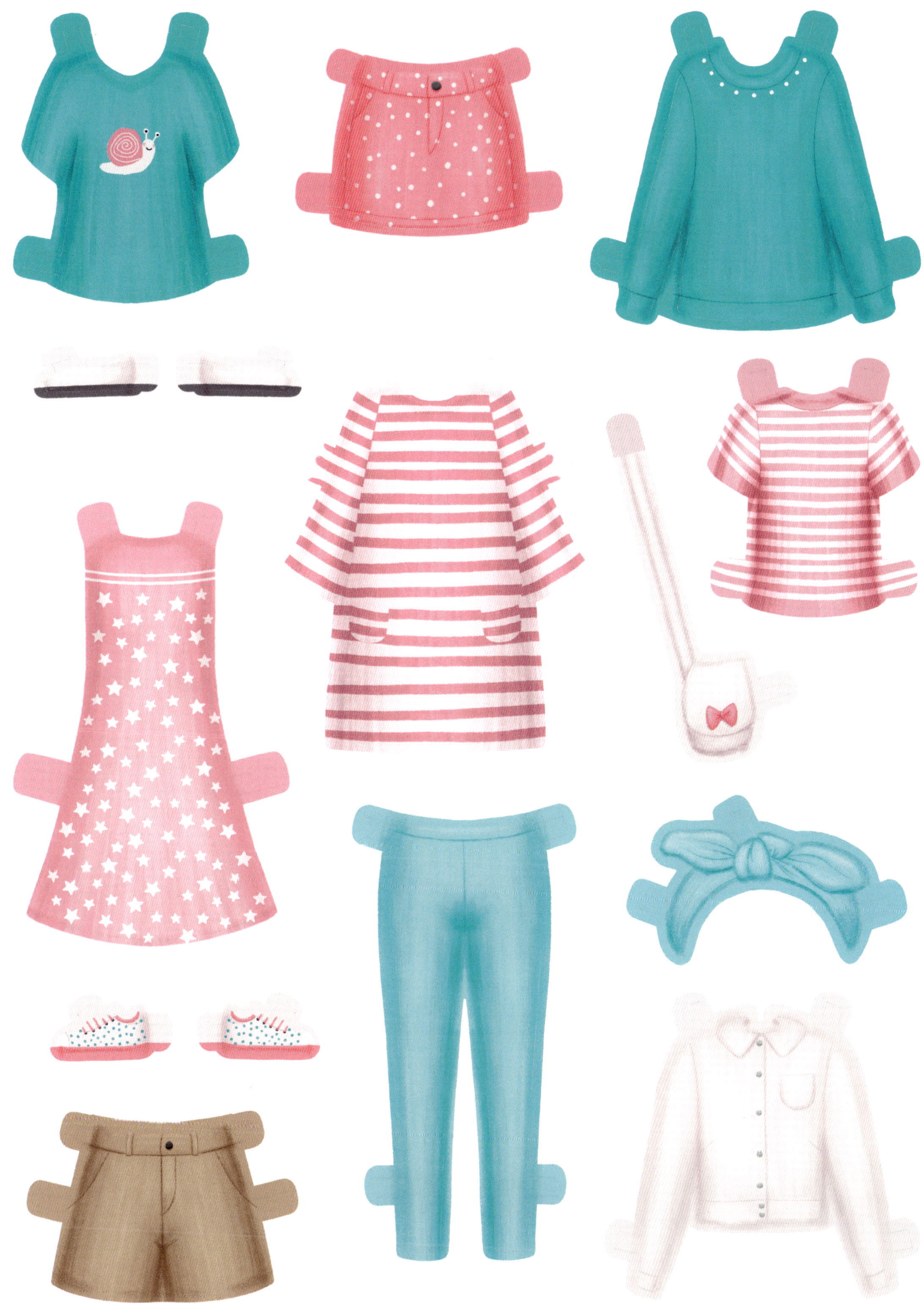

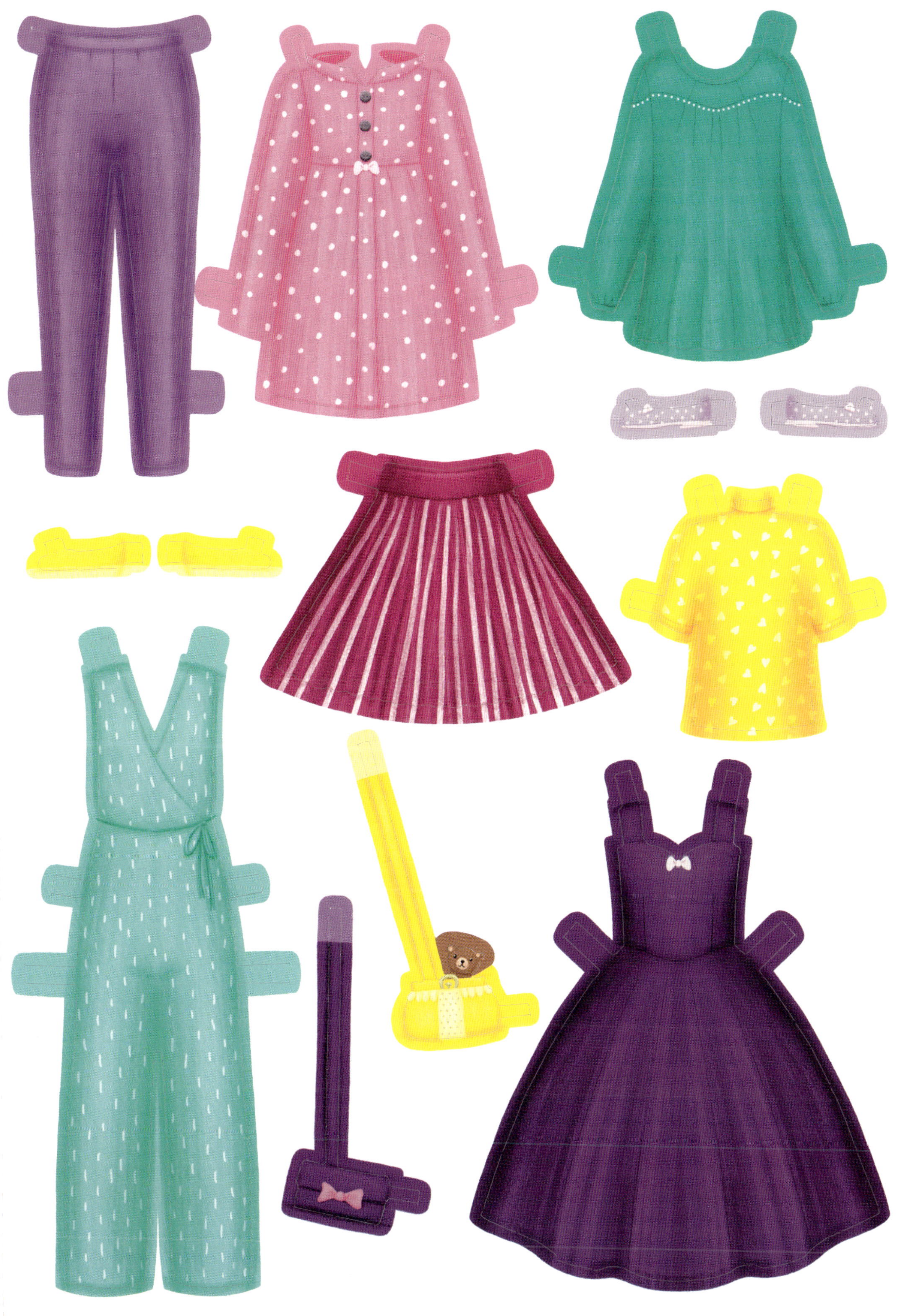

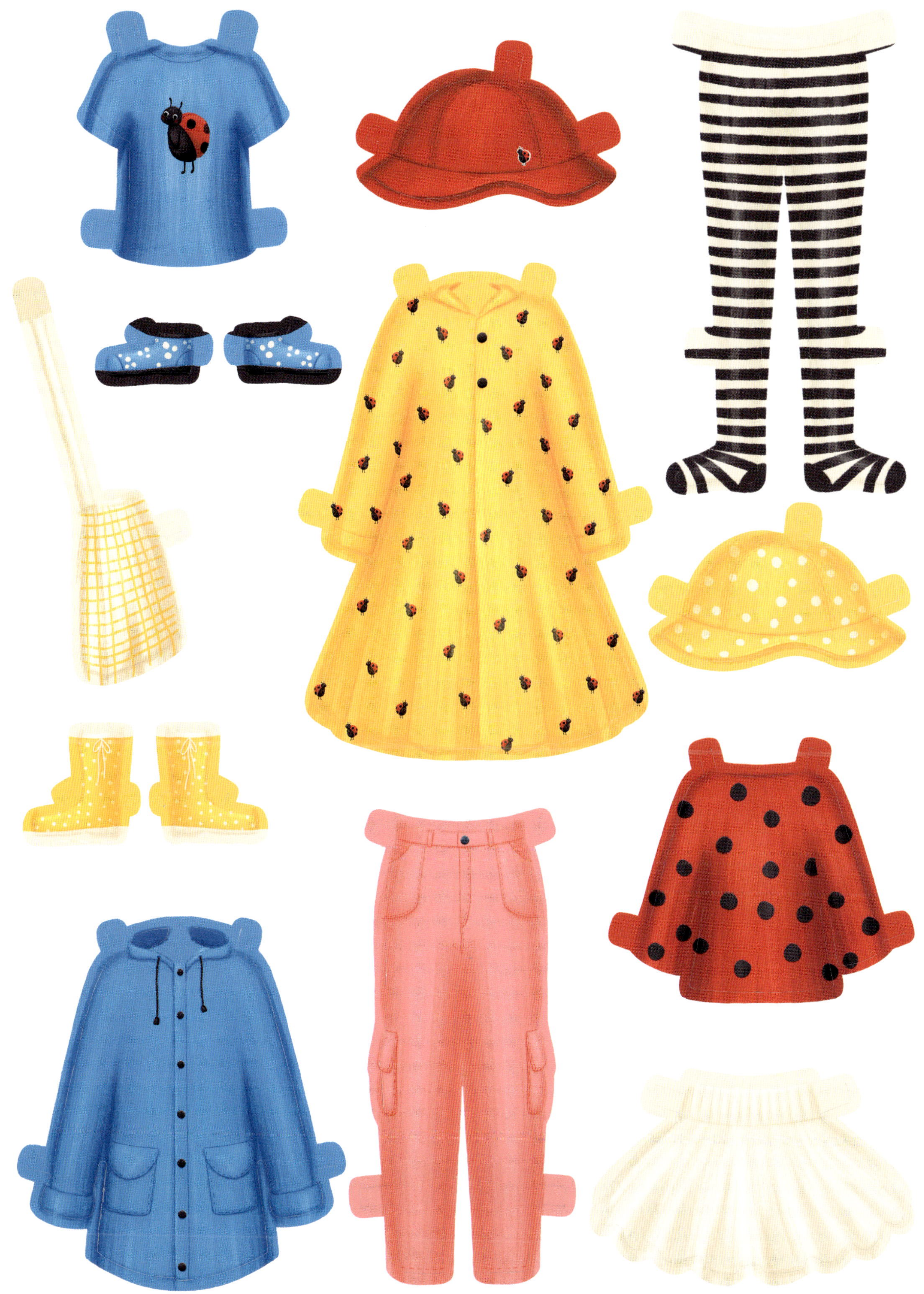

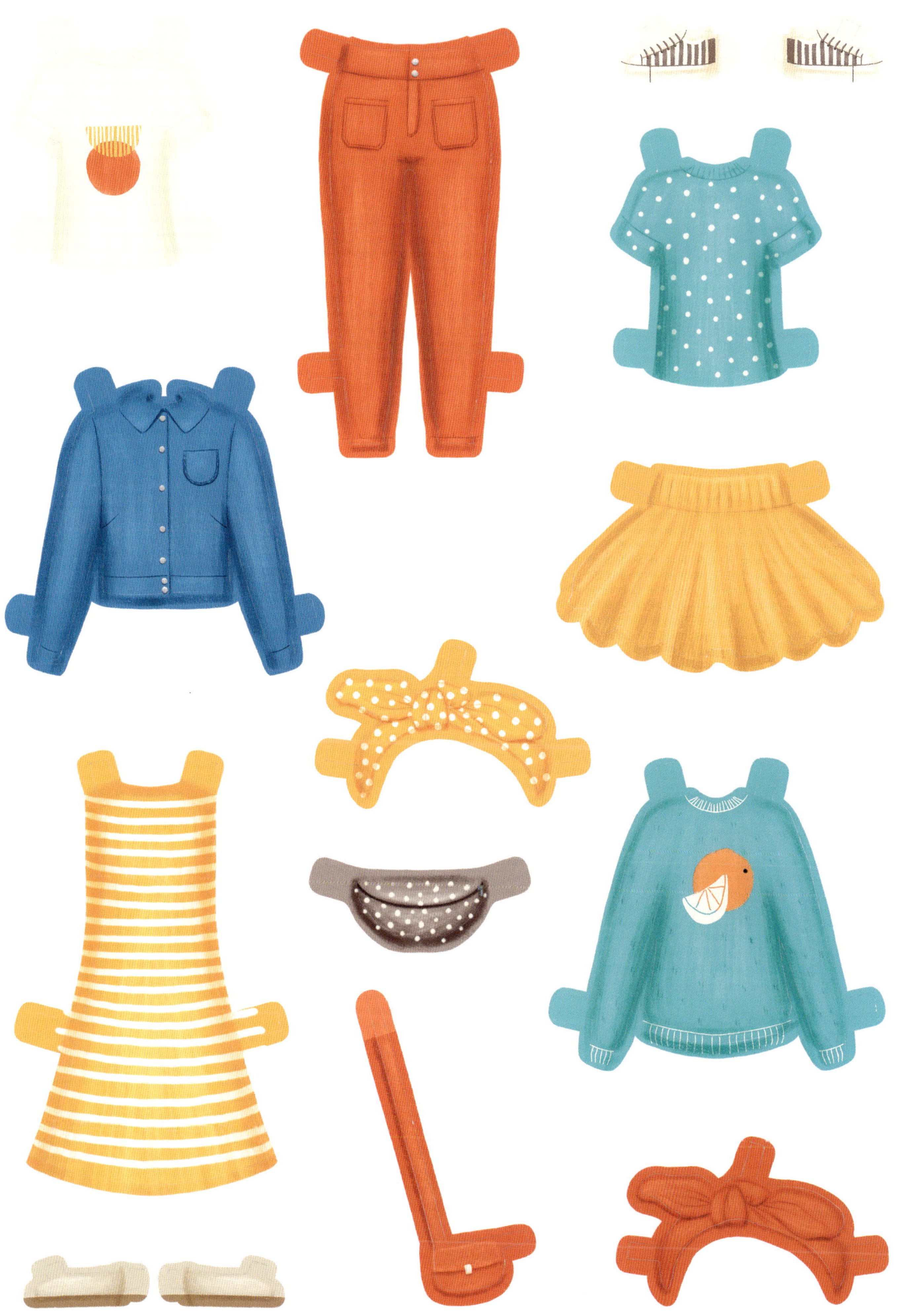

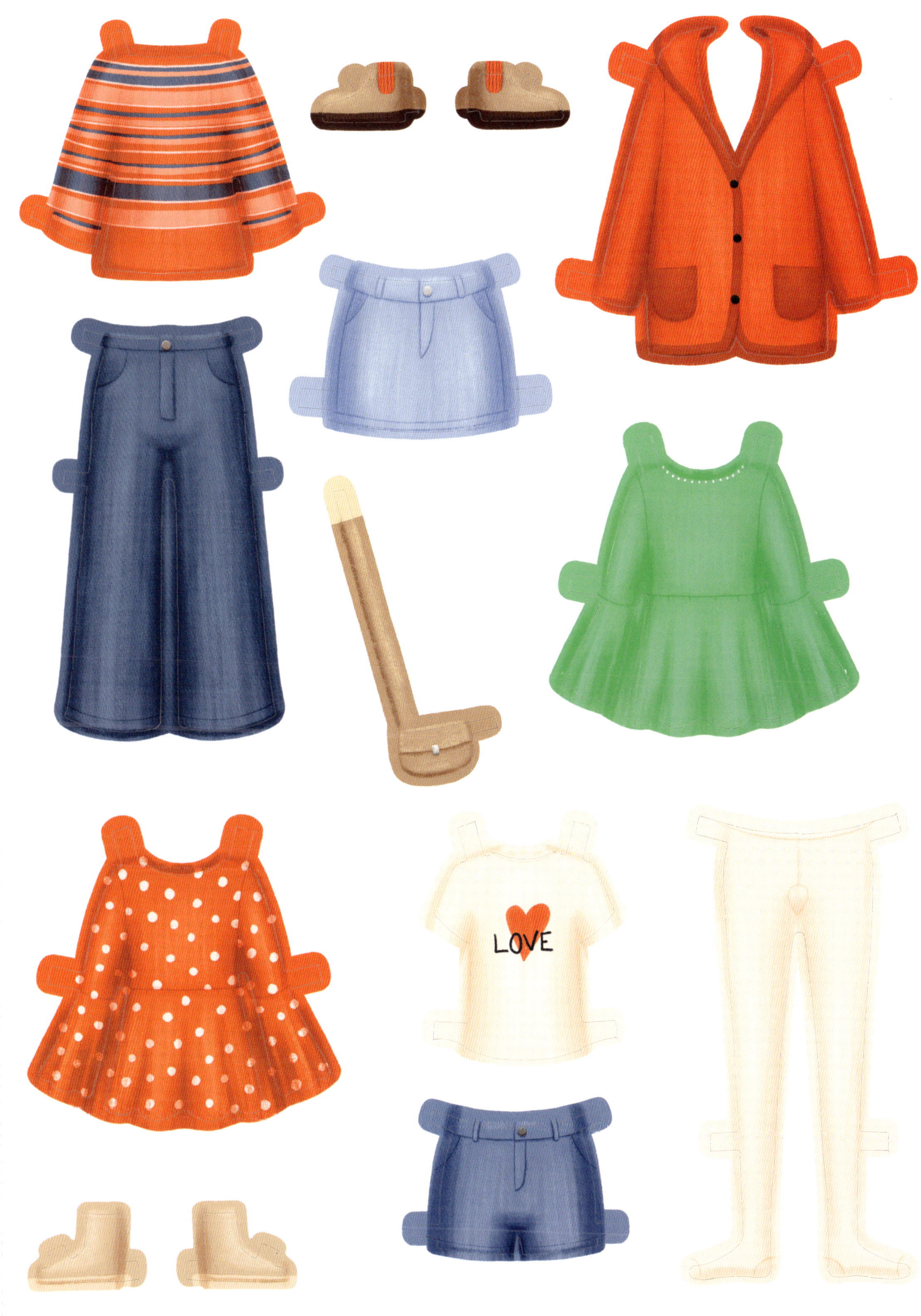
LOVE

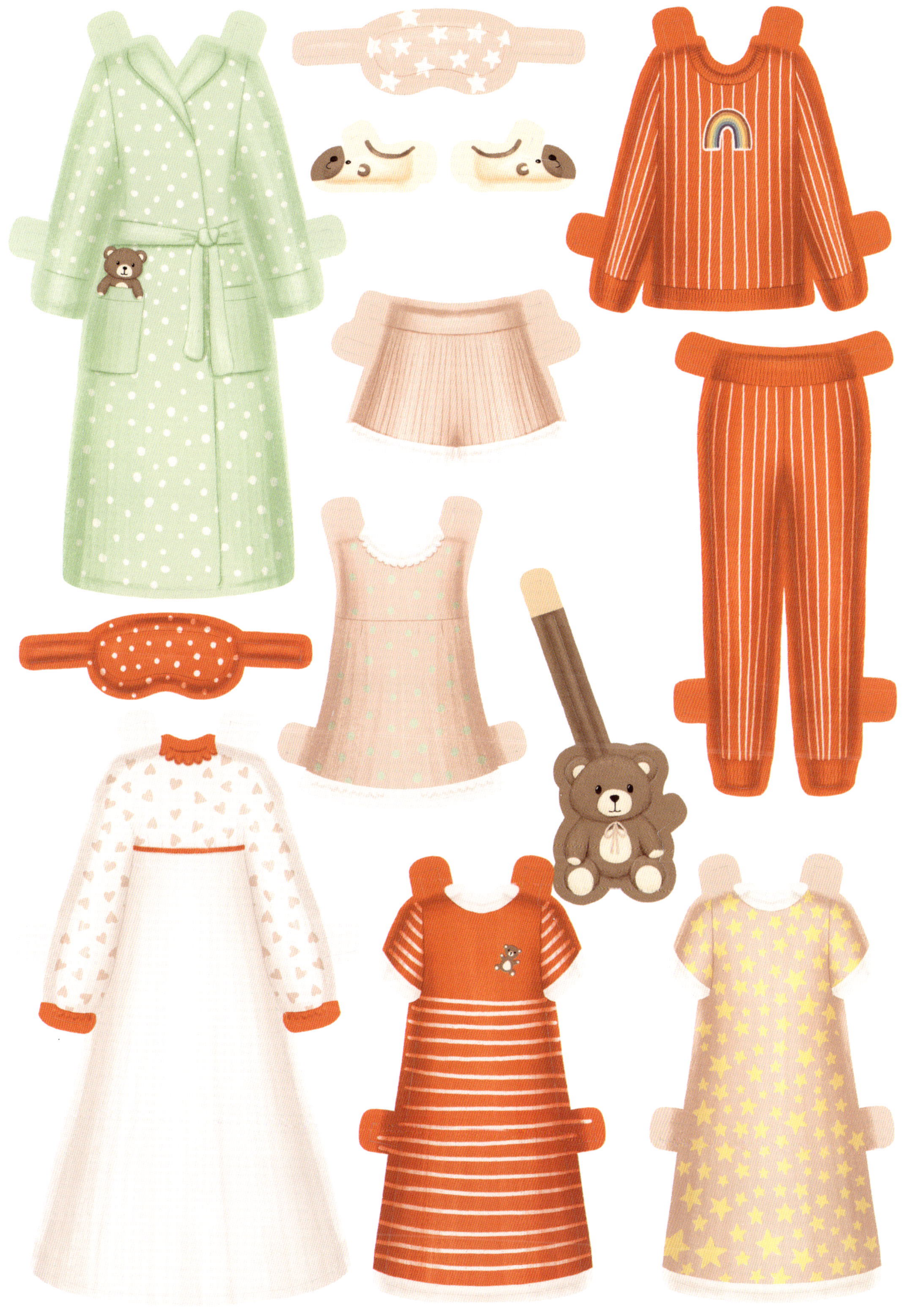

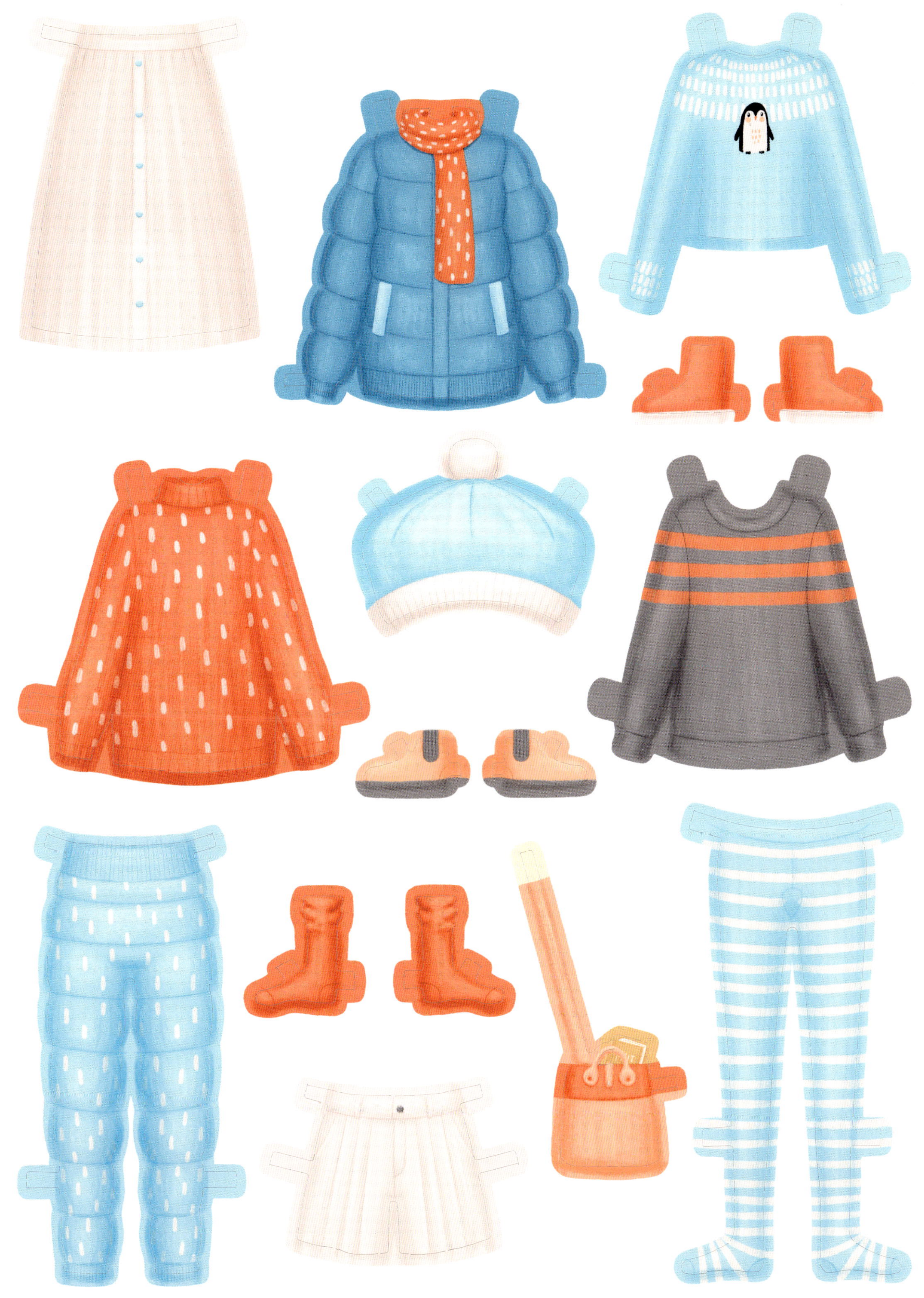

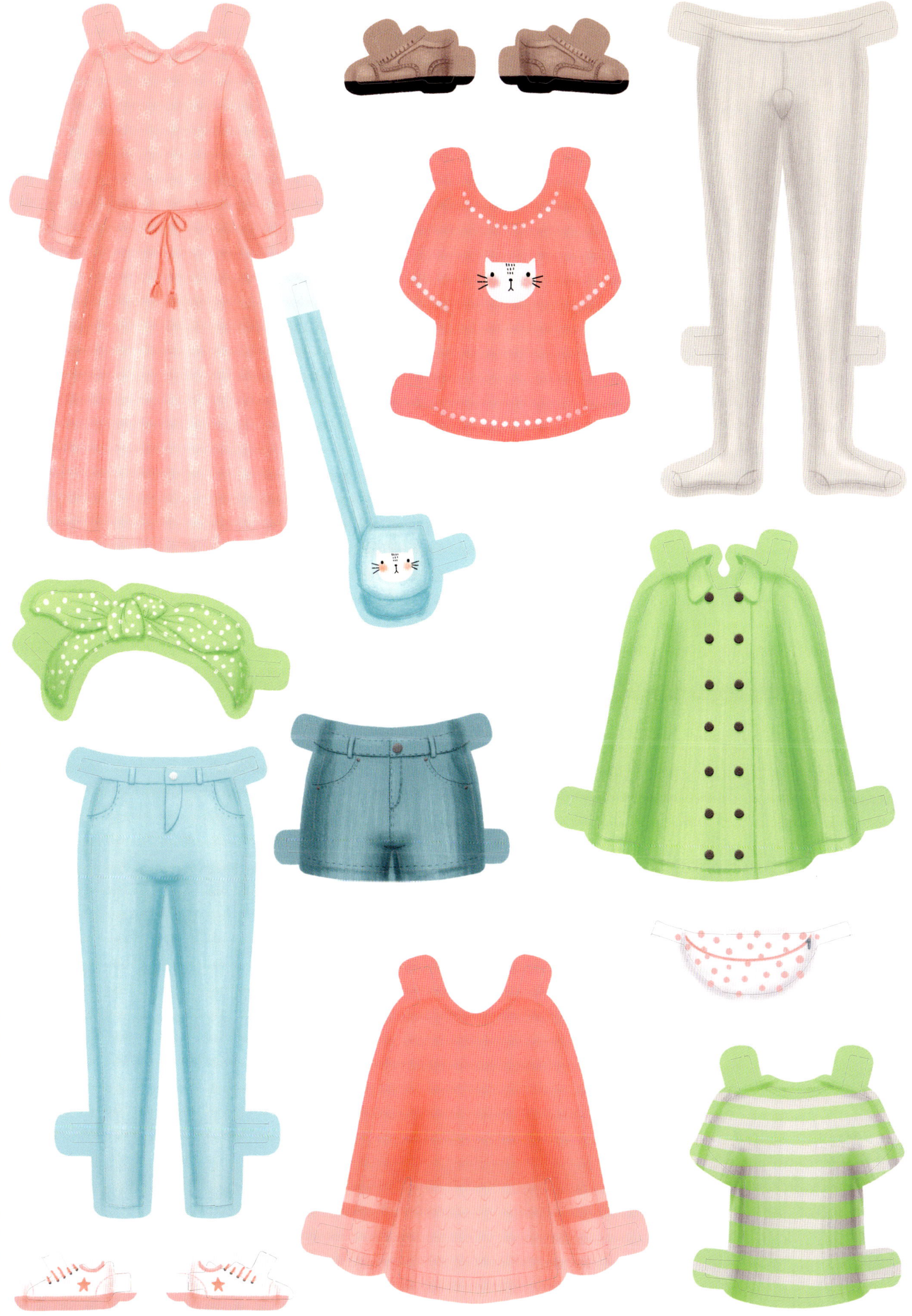

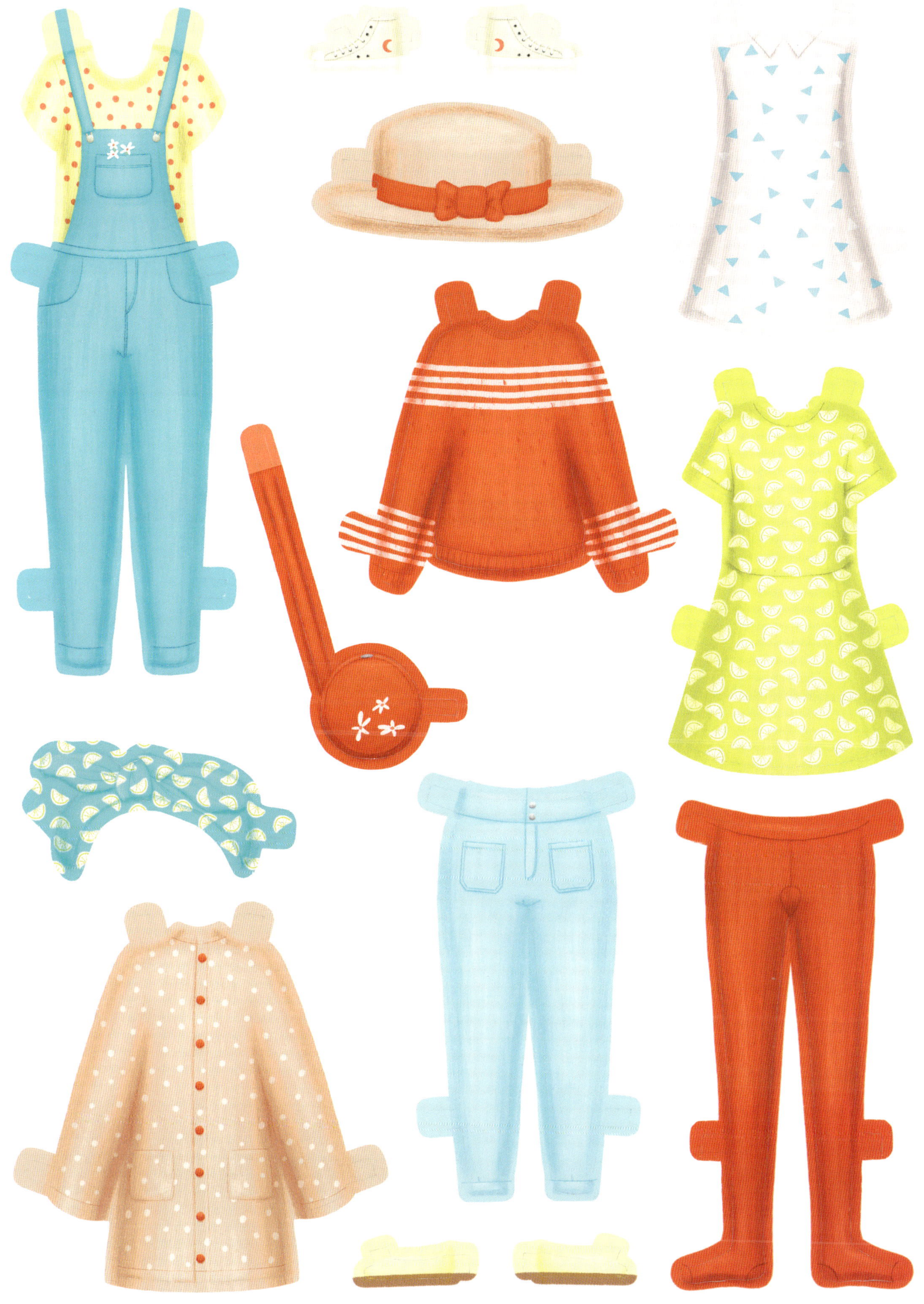

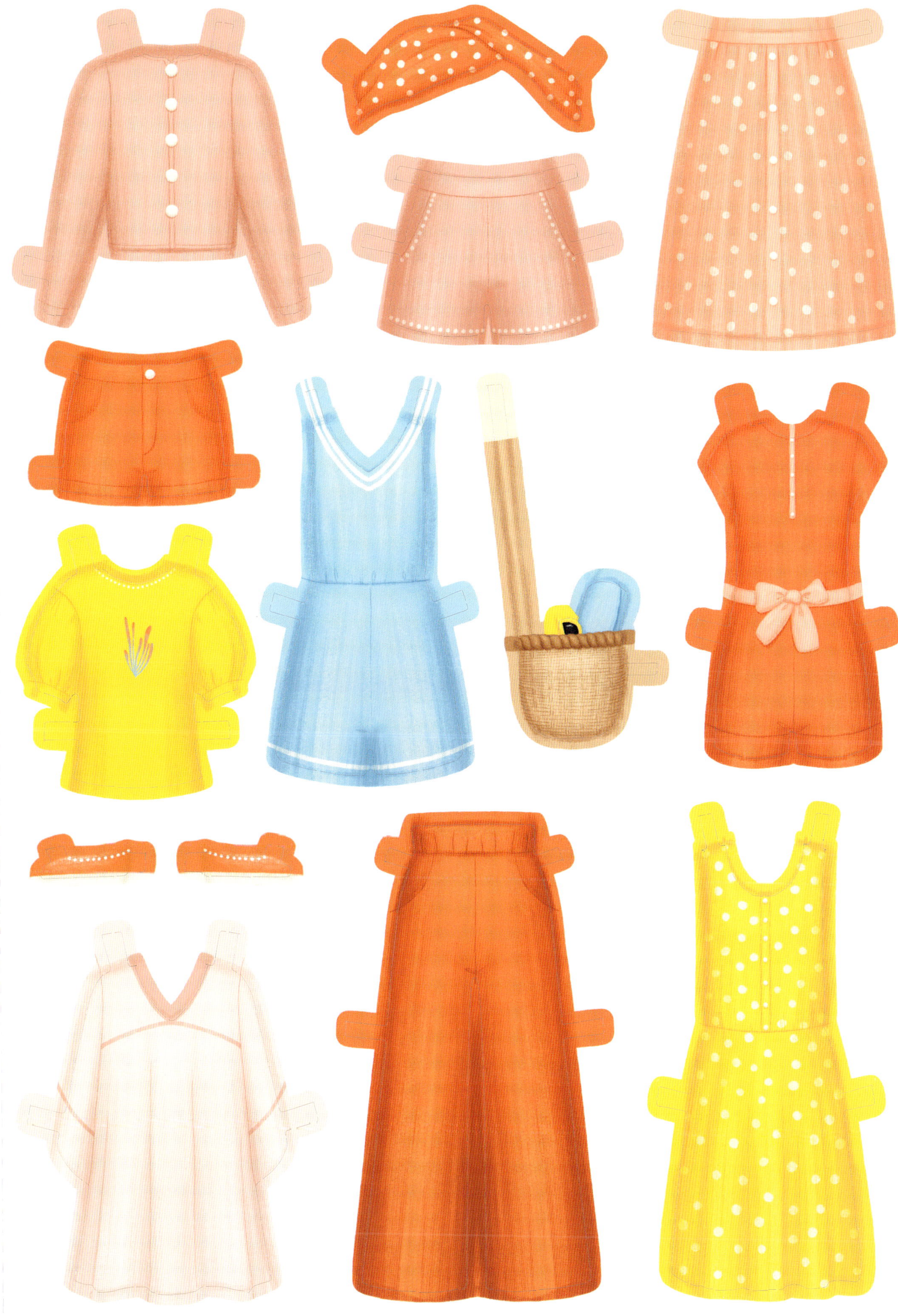

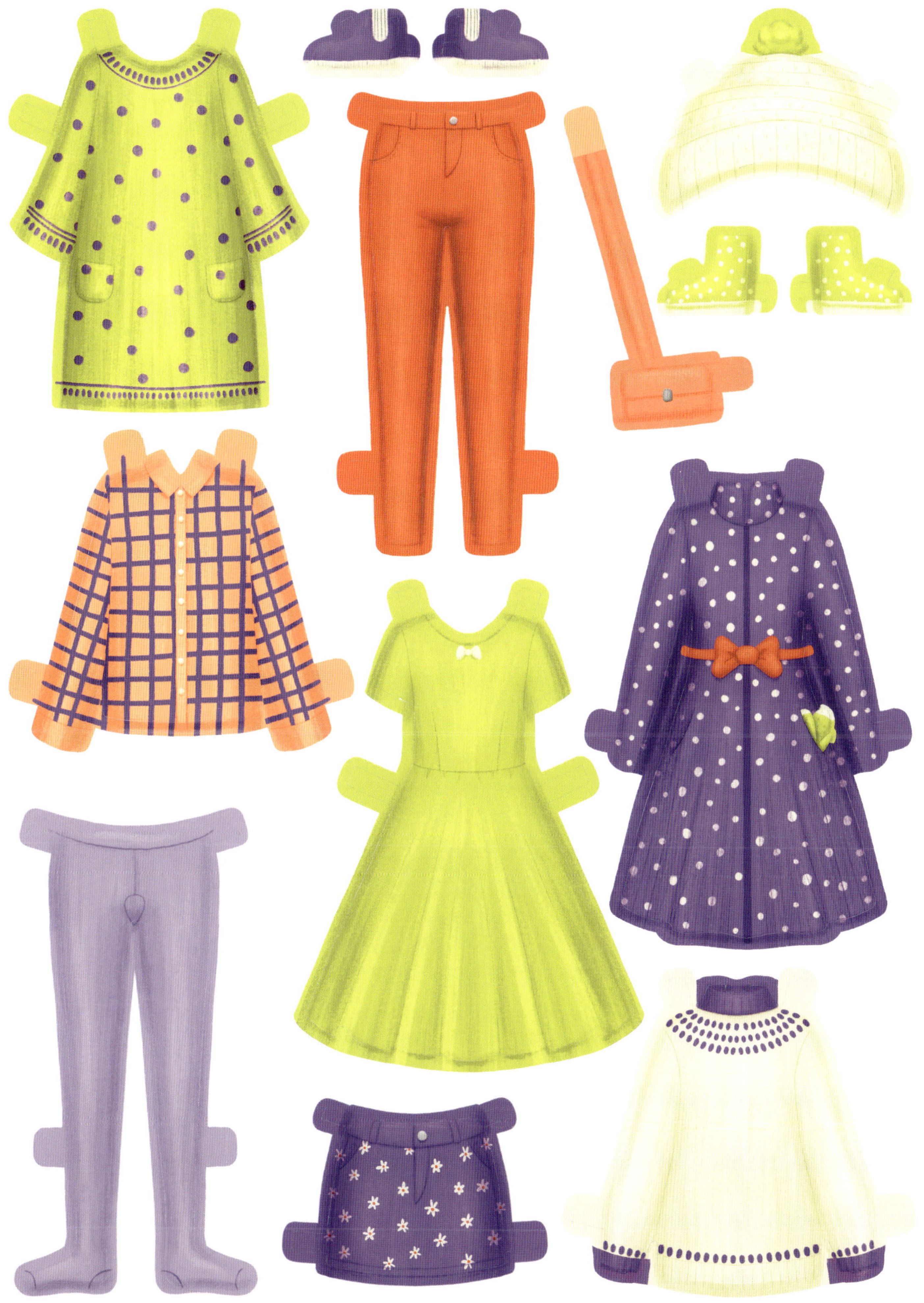

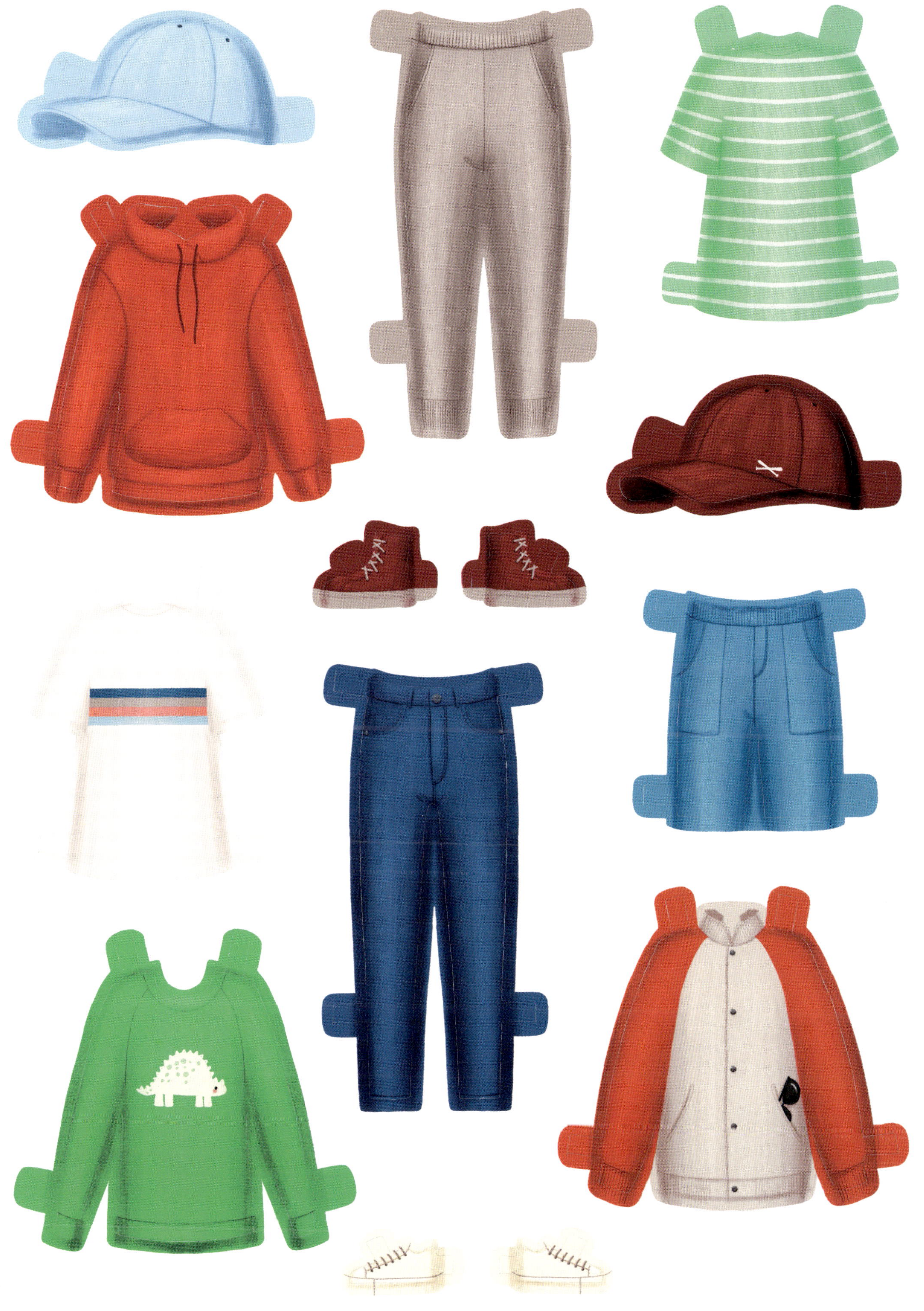

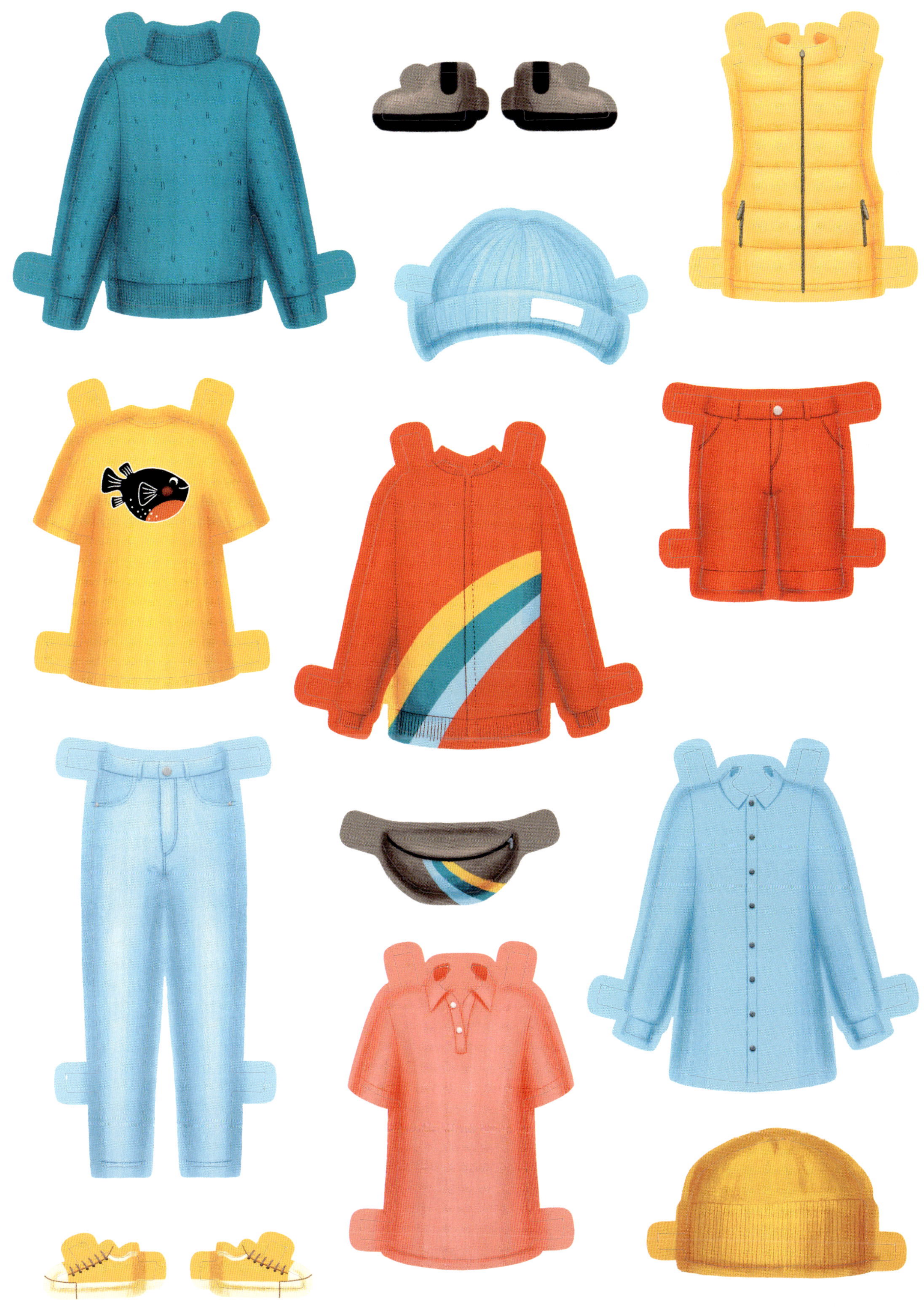

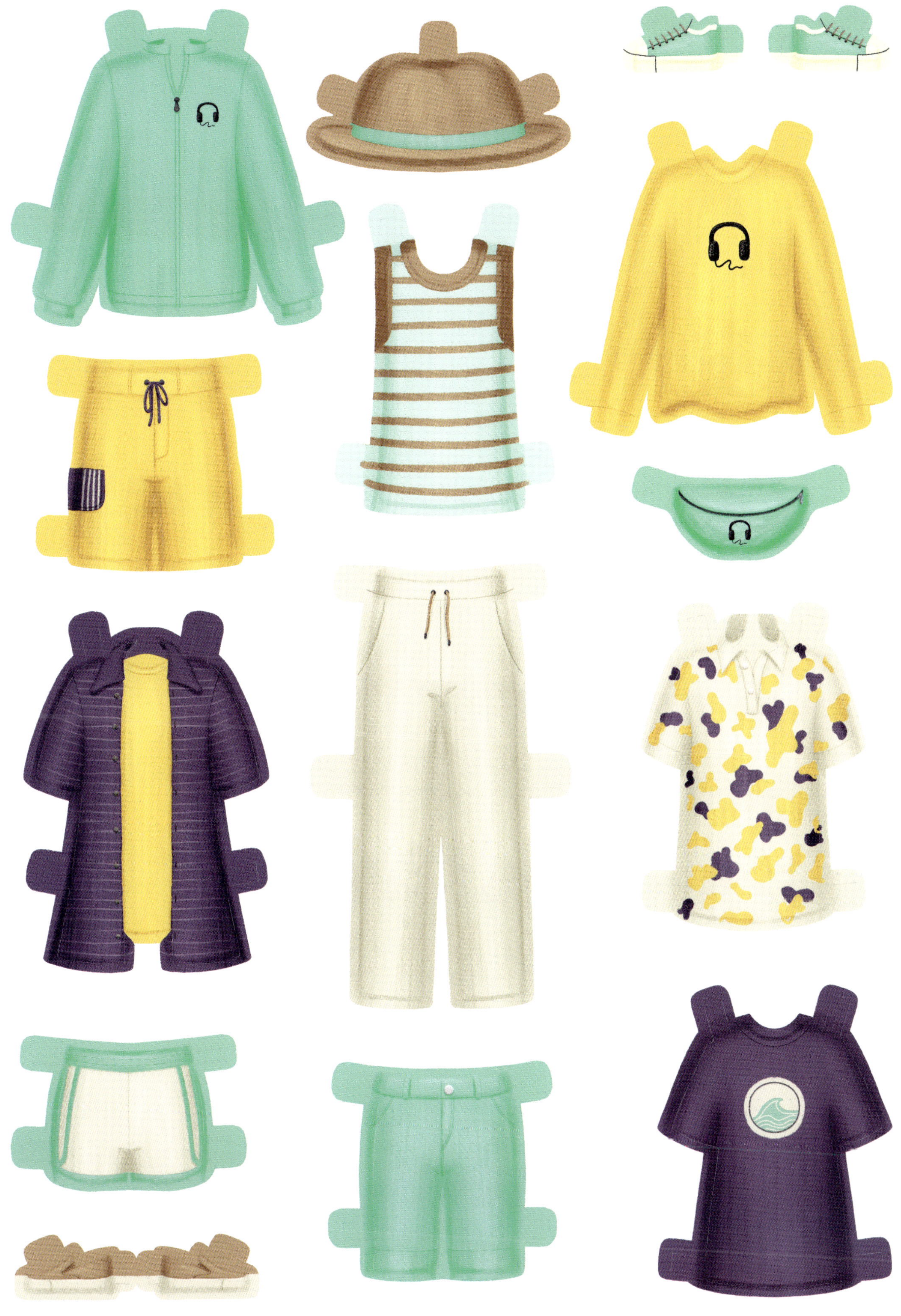

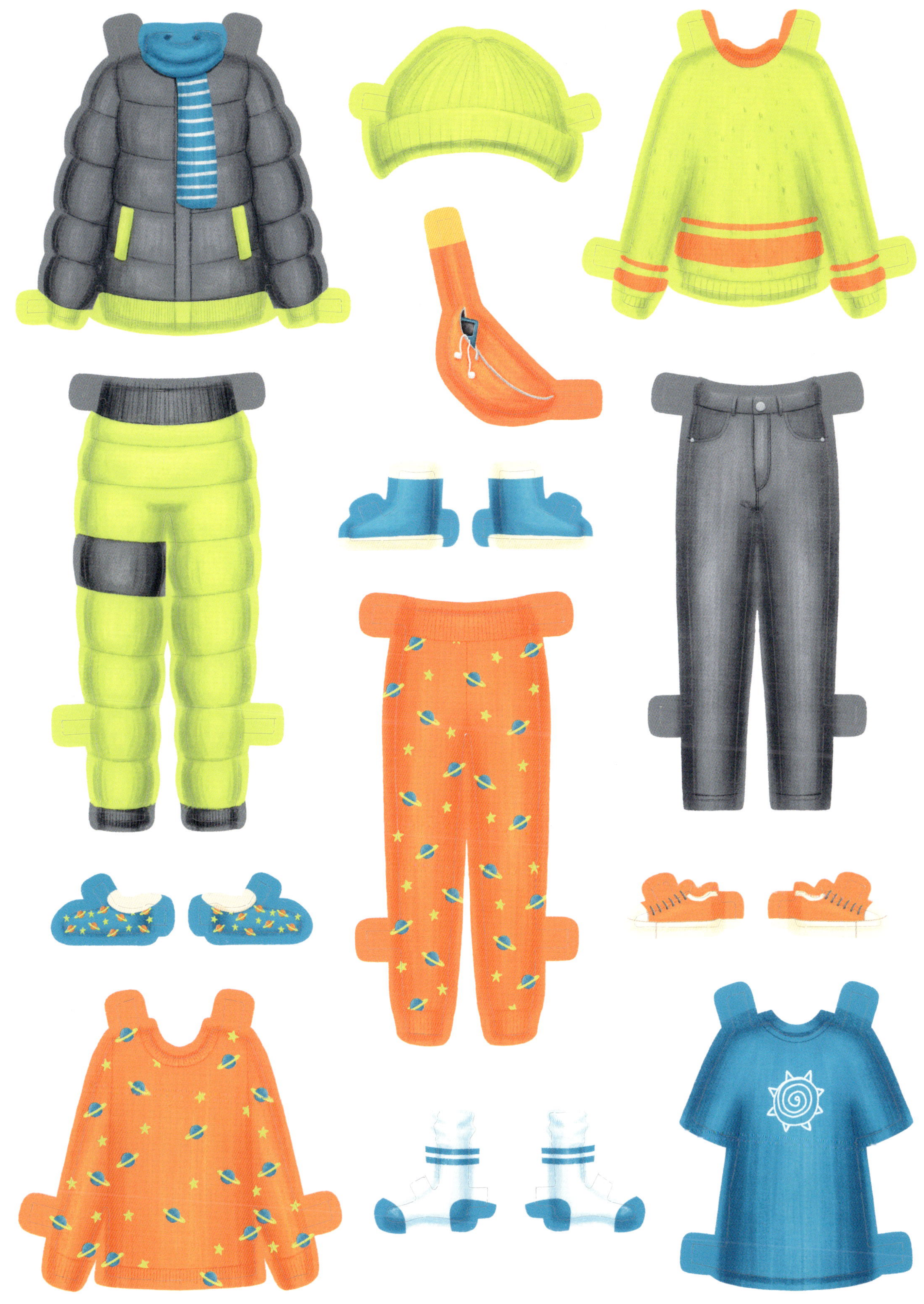